CAVALIER KING CHARLES SPANIEL

INTERPET
PUBLISHING

Introduction

Cavalier King Charles Spaniels are wonderful companion dogs. They are descended from the "small ladyes puppees" of the Royal English Court. Charles II adored this sweet and affectionate breed and even neglected the business of state to play with a "number of little spaniels."

Modern Cavaliers make wonderful family pets with their loving and sociable dispositions, and they are popular competitors at dog shows. They thrive on companionship and love a change of scene.

Although Cavaliers are prone to some serious health problems, responsible breeders now offer health-screened puppies for sale. A healthy Cavalier usually lives for between ten and twelve years.

Published by Interpet Publishing,
Vincent Lane, Dorking,
Surrey, RH4 3YX, UK.

ISBN 978 1 84286 246 9

Printed and bound in China

The information and recommendations in this book are given without any guarantees on behalf of the author and publisher, who disclaim any liability with the use of this material.

Contents

1 THE HISTORY OF THE CAVALIER KING CHARLES SPANIEL

The Cavalier King Charles Spaniel is descended from the King Charles Spaniel but is now a separate breed from this slightly smaller dog. These sweet toy dogs were known as "small ladyes puppees" that were wonderful lap and companion dogs. Unusually, Henry VIII allowed court ladies to have these "small spanyells" that were also known as "comforters" and "Spaniells gentle." Henry's daughter Mary Tudor and her husband Philip of Spain were painted with a little spaniel of this type playing at their feet. The first

ABOVE: *The King Charles Spaniel is distinguished from the Cavalier by its short face and smaller size.*
LEFT: *The Duke of Marlborough and family, with a Blenheim spaniel (19th century).*

7

written description of the Cavalier King Charles Spaniel dates back to 1570. Tragically, when Mary Queen of Scots was beheaded in 1587 at the order of Henry's other daughter, Elizabeth I a little black and white spaniel ran out from under her skirts, loyal to the very end. Mary was said to have acquired these toy spaniels when she was living in France as the wife of the Dauphin (the heir to the French throne). Elizabeth I's physician Dr. Johannes Caius was also the author of one of the world's first dog books, De Canibus Britannicus. The book catalogued all of the dog breeds of the time and Caius included the "Spaniell gentle or comforter - a delicate, neat and pretty kind of dog ... chamber companions, pleasant play fellows." Caius also maintained that cuddling

these little spaniels had the power to cure stomach ache. These dogs had long, pointed muzzles and looked quite different from the dogs of today.

It was during the reigns of Kings Charles I and II that the breed earned its royal nomenclature and became firm favourite at the royal court. Their popularity with the aristocracy ensured that these little toy dogs were painted by many of the most famous portrait painters of the period, appearing in works by Van Dyck, Titian, Lely, Gainsborough, Romney and Reynolds. Legend has it that King Charles was rarely seen without a few of these little dogs and it is said that the dogs were

ABOVE: *The Cavalier King Charles Spaniel has a long history as a royal favourite.*

ABOVE: *The Blenheim, or tan and white, Cavalier is the more widely available colouring.*

given permission to enter any public building (even Parliament) and the royal parks. This edict is still in force today. The rather frivolous Charles II was even criticised by Samuel Pepys for "playing with his dogs all the while" and neglecting the business of the kingdom. Evidently, the King even "suffered them to pup" in his bedroom. The other famous diarist of the

period, John Evelyn, said that Charles "took delight in having a number of little spaniels follow him and lie in his bedchamber." Ultimately, the King died in bed, surrounded by a dozen of his beloved little spaniels. These King Charles Spaniels were small and fine boned with domed heads, short muzzles, pointed noses, high set ears and almond ears. They looked very

ABOVE: *Queen Victoria with Flash, her Cavalier.*

much like their modern counterparts although our later dogs are a little larger, taller and have flatter heads with longer muzzles. Charles' brother King James II was also a great adherent of the dogs. When he was shipwrecked off the Scottish coast in 1613 and forced to abandon ship James asked the crew to "save the dogs" and as an afterthought, his son the Duke of Monmouth. But as the English Stuart kings gave way to the Dutch William and his English wife Mary Stuart in the late seventeenth century, these toy spaniels fell out of favour in these more austere and less flamboyant times and were replaced by pugs in royal favour.

This led to spaniels being bred with shorter muzzles. These dogs are now known as King Charles Spaniels, or "Charlies" rather than Cavaliers.

Although they had lost their pre-eminence at court, spaniels retained their favoured status at the Duke of Marlborough's "court" at the magnificent Blenheim Palace. This magnificent country house was to have a very important place in the history of the breed. The Blenheim spaniels were a special strain of red and white dogs that were particularly favoured by this noble family. Today, Blenheim colouring is one of the four recognised colours of the breed. These dogs have rich chestnut-coloured markings on a pearly white coat. These markings include a spot or lozenge of chestnut fur on top of the dog's head. The legend is that while Sarah, the Duchess of Marlborough was anxiously waiting to hear about her husband's triumph at the Battle of Blenheim, she repeatedly pressed her thumb onto the head of her pregnant spaniel. All five puppies were born with the "print" of her thumb between their ears and the mark (known as the Blenheim spot) has been worn by Blenheim spaniels ever since. The dogs were well known for their sporting ability and as lady's lap dogs. The Marlborough family were often painted with their Blenheim spaniels. One of these Blenheim spaniels appears in a 1665 portrait of Charles II's sister Henrietta of Orleans, which was painted by Pierre Mignard. She cuddles the little dog on her lap. In 2010, Blenheim Palace held a special show for both Cavaliers and King Charles Spaniels.

The royal connection with these dogs survived into the nineteenth century, when Queen Victoria's favourite dog was the famous tricolour (black, chestnut and white) spaniel, Dash. But Sir Edwin Landseer's portrait of the dog shows him to be rather more modern in type than Henrietta's dog, with his big round eyes and flattened skull. Landseer also painted a Blenheim spaniel in his 1845 picture Cavalier Pets. When Dash died, Queen Victoria wrote his touching epitaph, "Here lies Dash, the favourite spaniel of Her Majesty Queen Victoria, by whose command this memorial was erected. He died on the 20th of December 1840 in his ninth year. His attachment was without selfishness, his playfulness without malice, his fidelity without deceit. Reader, if you would live beloved and die regretted, profit by the example of Dash." In fact, Dash must

ABOVE: *Cavaliers are sociable dogs and if you can keep two of them they will enjoy the company.*

have been a typical spaniel.

By the end of Victoria's reign, the old type of longer-nosed toy spaniel had almost completely disappeared. These short-nosed dogs remained popular until 1926 when the wealthy American spaniel fan, Roswell Eldridge of New York offered a prize of £25 for the re-introduction of "Old Type" Stuart/Blenheim spaniels with longer noses and flattened skulls, as seen in the pictures of the Cavalier period. Eldridge's prize money was offered for five years. The famous Blenheim spaniel Ann's Son won the prize money between 1926 and 1930, and this dog was to become very important in the history of the breed as he became the ancestor of all modern Cavalier King

Charles Spaniels. The bitch Waif Julia was another winner of the prize. But little had been achieved as the prize money ended and the Kennel Club declined to register these long-nosed dogs as a separate breed. Eldridge himself had died in 1928.

Despite this setback, a dedicated Cavalier King Charles Spaniel Club was founded in 1928. The name was chosen to distinguish the dogs from the shorter-faced toy spaniels. The club immediately drew up a breed standard for Cavaliers, using paintings of the original dogs and contemporary animals of this type, like Ann's Son. As well as a strict description of the ideal Cavalier, the dogs were also expected to be "active, sporting and fearless."

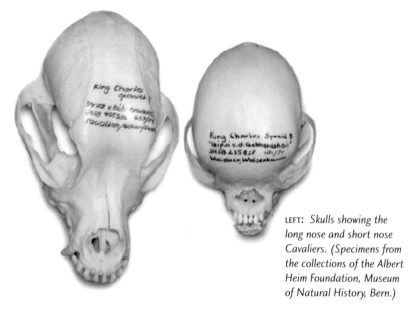

LEFT: *Skulls showing the long nose and short nose Cavaliers. (Specimens from the collections of the Albert Heim Foundation, Museum of Natural History, Bern.)*

A tall order for a little dog! It was also laid down that the breed should be as natural as possible, with no trimming or "carving."

Cavaliers struggled to even survive during World War II when many dogs of all types were destroyed because of the shortness of food and supplies. The famous Ttiweh kennel was reduced to just three Cavaliers, and just six dogs of the type were left by the end of the conflict. These six dogs are the forebears of all modern Cavaliers. These dogs were Ann's Son, Wizbang Timothy, Carlo of Ttiweh, Duce of Braemore, Kobba of Kuranda and Aristide of Ttiweh. Unfortunately, this tiny gene pool has resulted in some modern Cavaliers being affected by some serious and life-threatening genetic illnesses.

As the number of Cavaliers gradually built up after the war, the British Kennel Club finally recognized the breed in 1945. This meant that Cavaliers could now compete in a breed championship. The breed's first recognized champion was Daywell Roger. By this time, Cavaliers had become an extremely popular breed that regularly appeared in the top five most popular breeds in Britain. The breed went from strength to strength and became popular contestants at Crufts. In 1963 history was made when Mrs. F. Cryer won the Toy Group at Crufts with her bitch Champion Amelia of Laguna. A Cavalier was also the first

ABOVE: *Daywell Roger.*

toy dog to win Best in Show at Crufts in 1973. This was Alansmere Aquarius a descendant of the famous Ann's Son. This win caused a huge spike in Cavalier popularity.

The British Cavalier King Charles Spaniel Club continues to campaign for the health and welfare of the breed, and conducted an international Cavalier Health Census in 2013. The club also sponsors research into Cavalier health problems.

Cavaliers became increasingly popular as time went on. They were such a convenient size, happy to lead many different lifestyles, and didn't need any trimming. They were also family friendly and made wonderful companions for single people. This popularity led to some inappropriate breeding but the quality of the Cavalier line managed to survive. The breed also continued to make friends in high places. Princess Margaret had a Cavalier called Rowley while President Reagan and his wife Nancy were often

ABOVE: *Cavaliers are adaptable and friendly, making them a popular pet.*

photographed with their Blenheim.

Cavaliers also began to get popular in America; the first Cavaliers arrived in the 1940s. Mrs. Sally Lyons Brown of Kentucky fell in love with English Cavaliers and took one home with her in 1952. Mrs. Lyons Brown founded the first American Cavalier Club in 1954, the Cavalier King Charles Spaniel Club. At the time there were only around a dozen dogs in the United States, so it was a pretty exclusive club! Mrs. Lyons Brown and her sister-in-law Trudy Brown Albrecht became tireless ambassadors for the breed and bred

some lovely dogs. The club held its first National Speciality show in 1962, but consistently declined recognition from the American Kennel Club. At this stage there were still only around 64 Cavaliers that had been born in America. A splinter group subsequently formed the American Cavalier King Charles Club and decided to accept Kennel Club recognition in 1995. At this point Cavaliers were finally recognized as an official breed in America, and an official breed standard was adopted.

2 CHOOSING YOUR CAVALIER PUPPY

Cavalier King Charles Spaniel puppies are adorable but getting any dog is a serious undertaking and you should be sure that you really want a dog (any dog) and that a Cavalier is the right dog for you. Toy dogs are wonderful companions and are very flexible, happy to live in town or country. The issue of having time to exercise and give your dog the companionship he deserves is particularly critical to Cavalier ownership. Although your Cavalier will not need particularly long walks, these dogs thrive on companionship and love a change of scene.

Companionship is crucial to the happiness of your Cavalier, and he

certainly would not enjoy being left alone for long periods of time. No dog should be treated like this, as loneliness will almost certainly lead to bad and destructive behaviour. If you know you will need to leave your dog for any regular periods, you should seriously consider having two dogs. As Cavaliers are quite delicate, they might not be the best choice for a family with boisterous young children who may inadvertently hurt the little dogs. This consideration aside, Cavaliers make wonderful family pets with their sweet and mild dispositions. They also fit in well with other dogs and even cats! They are moderately easy to train, and want to please. Their most endearing quality is their sociability and their intense love of cuddles and games.

BELOW: *Cavaliers have sweet and mild dispositions.*

Dog or Bitch?

ABOVE: *Breeders often wish to keep a bitch to breed from making a dog easier to buy.*

The personality differences between male and female Cavaliers are quite subtle, and both make excellent pets. Both male and female Cavaliers are equally affectionate but some people do not want to be bothered with a female's half-yearly seasons. In fact, bitches usually keep themselves very clean and their seasons are very little trouble. Spayed bitches may become fat and get too much coat. Some Cavalier males like to mark their territory, even indoors so it may take a little more effort to perfect their toilet training. Male Cavaliers are very rarely aggressive and as adults they often have very handsome coats with luxuriant feathering.

There are advantages and disadvantages for both male and female Cavaliers, but it is usually easier to buy a dog as breeders tend to keep their bitches to breed from.

Pet or Show Dog?

ABOVE: *Always go to a reputable breeder to buy your puppy.*

Cavaliers should first and foremost be bought as companion dogs, whether or not you would like to show your dog. Only some Cavaliers enjoy being show dogs, even really good looking animals. If you really want to show your Cavalier, you may be better buying your dog from a specialist show kennel who will sell their dogs at around six months of age, rather than as young puppies. This will mean that you can see the realistic potential of your dog, as you will be able to see how their adult teeth have come in, and if their testicles have descended. These dogs are likely to be rather more expensive as the breeder will have had to outlay more on veterinary care, inoculations and food. If you want to buy a show dog,

it may be better to buy your Cavalier from a kennel with famous bloodlines and a track record of show success. It would also help if you had researched the breed standard and had some idea of what you should be looking for.

If you are looking for a pet, the main thing is to buy a healthy and happy dog with a pretty face.

As with all puppies, it is very important to buy a puppy from a reputable breeder rather than a puppy farm or pet shop. This is no time to look for a bargain, and you should get to know the real current price for a healthy, well-sourced Cavalier puppy. You should also ask to see proof of health testing on the parents of the puppies for genetically transmitted health problems, especially their eyes and hearts. Unfortunately, Cavaliers are prone to several genetic illnesses that you should take all care to avoid. A failure to do this could result in misery and heartache at a later date. You should make every effort to buy your puppy from health screened stock. There are three main conditions that are currently screened for in Cavaliers: Mitral Valve Disease (MVD), Syringomyelia (SM), and various eye conditions. You may well wish to ask a breeder what sort of lifespan can be expected from his stock.

ABOVE: *If you are looking for a family pet you just want a healthy dog with a pretty face.*

RIGHT: *If you are looking for a show dog, the breeder will help you assess breed points.*

19

ABOVE: *Syringomyelia is a condition that can affect Cavaliers.*

Considering Health Issues

MITRAL VALVE DISEASE

Very sadly, mitral valve disease is the leading cause of death for Cavaliers around the world. It affects around half of Cavaliers before the age of five, and almost all ten-year-old Cavaliers will have the condition. However, many dogs live a normal lifespan with the condition. The illness causes the degeneration of the heart's mitral valve. Your vet should check your Cavalier's heartbeat at his annual check up and he may then refer the dog for further investigation or a scan. No dog who has developed the condition before he or she reaches five years of age should be bred from.

SYRINGOMYELIA

Syringomyelia is another condition that can affect Cavaliers. The disease results in fluid filled cavities in the spinal cord. The symptoms can be mild or severe, but the first sign is often when a Cavalier starts to scratch the air near its neck as it feels twinges in that region. It is said that the condition results from the Cavalier's small skull not having enough space for the entire cerebellum, which is pushed out of the back of the skull. The condition is usually diagnosed between the ages of 6 months and 3 years, often by an MRI scan. The illness can progress and result in serious pain or disability. Most dogs are treated for the condition with drugs, but surgical options may also be offered.

EYE PROBLEMS

Around 30% of Cavaliers are affected by various genetic eye problems. These include cataracts, dry eye syndrome, corneal dystrophy, distichiasis, microphthalmia, retinal degeneration, cherry eye and retinal dysplasia. Your vet should also check your Cavalier's eyes at his annual check up to make sure that none of these conditions has developed.

ABOVE: *Eye problems can affect your Cavalier so your vet show examine his eyes at the annual check-up.*

BELOW: *A happy, healthy puppy.*

21

Puppy or Older Dog?

One of the great things about adopting a grown-up Cavalier is that you are probably giving a home to a dog that really needs one. There are many rescue organisations with dogs available in Britain, the United States and Canada. There will also be advantages to you. Your older dog may well be house trained (or nearly house trained!) and may also have been taught how to walk on the lead, and ride in the car. An older Cavalier may also be more appropriate for an elderly or infirm owner. You can also see exactly what you are getting in the way of temperament and size. The best way to find an older Cavalier may be through a breed rescue organisation. Dogs can end up in rescue kennels for many reasons, most of which are not any fault of the dog. For example, his owner may have died or become ill, or a dog bought for showing may not have reached the required standard. Breeding bitches and stud dogs may also have been retired and would hugely benefit from having a loving and relaxed home of their own. One of the great things about Cavaliers is that, because they are such lively and affectionate dogs, they will soon adapt to you and your lifestyle. An older dog might also find it easier if you are not at home all day and probably won't be as needy as a puppy.

Once you have decided what kind of Cavalier you would like to have, you need to find a highly regarded breeder. One of the best ways to do this is to contact a Cavalier breed club. Breed clubs often have lists of litters that have been bred by their members. If you can, it is highly desirable to meet the breeder before you decide to buy. A good breeder will want to know that you can offer a good home to one of their puppies and you can see the conditions in which your pup has been bred. Another good way of contacting breeders is to visit dog shows where Cavaliers are being shown. This would also give a wonderful opportunity of meeting some Cavaliers close up and seeing the different sexes, sizes, and colours of the breed. The UK Kennel Club also has the Assured Breeder Scheme where their members can offer litters on-line through their website. This is an excellent way of buying a dog for showing if that is your ambition.

But the very best way to find your puppy is by personal recommendation from someone who has already bought a puppy from a breeder. If you are looking for a Cavalier to be a loving pet and companion, you need to look for a puppy from an affectionate and healthy environment.

A good breeder will also want to make sure that they are placing their puppies in good homes and should ask many questions about your home environment and lifestyle. If they do not feel that you can offer one of their puppies a good home, they may even refuse to sell you one.

If you are lucky enough to find a litter that has the kind of pup you are looking for, It can be a great bonding experience to meet your future puppy a couple of times before you take him home with you. It will also give you a chance to meet the parents of your puppy (or the dam at least) and this will give you an idea of how your dog will develop. You can also keep an eye on him to make sure that he stays in good health before you pick him up. This should be at around eight weeks old. A good breeder will be happy to welcome you to see your puppy and will be pleased by your interest.

23

Choosing Your Puppy

ABOVE: *There is no point in selecting your puppy when he is less than five weeks old.*

PUPPY LAYETTE

Before you collect your puppy, you will need to equip yourself with some simple pup-friendly equipment. His requirements will include a bed, basket, or dog crate a puppy collar and lead, a grooming brush, safe, durable puppy-friendly toys and puppy food (as per the breeder's instructions). It is well worth investing in a special spaniel water bowl. These heavy earthenware pots are tapered towards the top to stop your Cavalier's ears falling into the water. Stainless steel dishes are ideal for their food and won't be chewed.

Once you have found a litter from which to choose your puppy you need to use some objectivity to choose the right dog for you. In fact, there's no point in looking at a litter prior to five weeks of age. You need to see the puppies on their feet before you can judge them properly. If possible, it would be great to see the puppies' mother and father. The main points

ABOVE: *The stainless steel dish is sturdy and ideal for food.*

ABOVE: *The earthenware dish is specially shaped to avoid the spaniel's ears flopping inside.*

to look for are your puppy's physical and behavioural health. So far as his physical health goes, there are several things that you should look out for. The puppy should have a good level of energy, and appear alert and interested in his surroundings. His eyes should be bright and clear without any crust or discharge, and he should be able to see a ball that rolls by slowly. He should look well fed, and have a little fat over his ribs. A healthy puppy's bottom should be free from faeces. His coat should be flat and glossy and not scurfy, dull or greasy. There should be no evidence of fleas or lice in his coat. He should be able to walk freely without any limping or discomfort. The puppy should be able to hear you if you clap behind his head.

So far as his behaviour goes, you should look for a puppy that seems to be interacting well with his littermates – playing nicely without being too assertive. The puppy should also be interested in playing with you and should approach you willingly. He should be happy about being handled, and let you cuddle him and touch him all over his body. If he remains calm and relaxed while you do this, he is likely to be easier to handle when he grows up. The most

ABOVE: *A puppy should be calm and relaxed when you handle him.*

desirable Cavalier temperament can coexist with other dogs, cats, birds, small children and guests. A passive but outgoing and happy puppy who can live comfortably with other species will be an easy dog to live with. A very boisterous or timid puppy will probably be the same when he grows up.

RIGHT: *Choose a puppy who plays nicely with his littermates.*

25

Preparing for Your Puppy

You will need to make some important preparations before your collect your puppy and bring him home. You need to decide where you want your puppy to sleep, eat and exercise and which parts of your house you will allow the puppy to go. Consistent behaviour on your part will help your puppy feel secure and settle down quickly, so start as you mean to go on. All dogs need to

ABOVE: *A puppy crate will be useful.*

have a routine and it is best to get this established as soon as possible.

Before you collect your puppy you must make sure that his new environment is free of any hidden hazards. Very importantly, your garden needs to be well fenced. A little Cavalier puppy needs only a tiny hole to squeeze through. Any openwork gates should have wire mesh attached, and any dangerous garden equipment should be put away. Ponds are a particular hazard for these little dogs. If they fall in, they may well be unable to climb out. Indoors, you must make sure that electrical cables and phone wires are concealed.

It is also a good idea to put away anything you really don't want to be chewed. You don't want to be telling off your new puppy on his first day in his new home. It might be a good idea to confine your small Cavalier to a metal or plastic puppy pen to keep him as safe as possible.

One of the most important things to decide is where your puppy is going to sleep. This is crucial as this is somewhere that your puppy needs to feel completely safe and secure. It should be a place that suits both you and the dog. The most important thing is that the sleeping area should be warm, dry and completely draught free.

Many owners prefer their new puppies to sleep in the kitchen or utility room as these rooms usually have washable floors. But you should not let him sleep in a confined space where there is a boiler in case of carbon monoxide leaks. You could also fence off a small area around the basket with his puppy pen so that your puppy won't be able to get into trouble in the night. A dog crate or cage can also make your dog feel comfortable and secure. If you leave the door open, your dog can also use the crate as his refuge during the day. Dog crates are also useful to keep your dog confined and safe during car journeys. You should never use the crate to punish your dog, as he should always want to go into it.

Although there are many different kinds of dog beds on the market, the simple plastic kidney-shaped baskets, which come in many different sizes and colours, are some of the most practical. They resist chewing and can be washed and disinfected. They can also be filled with cosy pads or mattresses on which the puppy can sleep comfortably. These mattress inserts can usually be washed in the washing machine. It's a good idea to buy two of these in case of accidents! An excellent idea is to replace the fabric softener in the washing cycle with a slug of disinfectant to make sure that any germs or bad smells are destroyed. Wicker baskets can be dangerous when chewed as the sharp sticks can damage the puppy's mouth or throat. Equally, bean bag beds can easily be chewed through and the polystyrene beans they contain are difficult to clean up. Dog duvets are equally prone to chewing.

DANGEROUS PLANTS FOR DOGS

Many house and garden plants are highly toxic to dogs and puppies, and you should be very careful to keep them away from your Cavalier at any age. Of course puppies are much more likely to chew unsuitable things, so you need to be particularly careful that they are not exposed to a whole list of dangerous plant materials including:

Aconites	Bluebells	Cocoa husks (used in garden mulches)	Onions
African Violets	Box wood		Ragwort
Apple seeds	Buttercups	Daffodil bulbs	Rhubarb
Apricot stones	Cherry stones	Elephant ears	Wild cherry
Crocuses	Christmas roses	Ivy	Yew
Avocado	Clematis	Mistletoe	

Collecting Your Puppy

The best age to collect your puppy is when he is around eight weeks old. When you arrange a time to pick him up from the breeder, a time around mid-morning is often the most convenient. This will give the puppy a good chance to feel at home by bedtime. He will be able to sniff around his new home, be cuddled by his new owners, eat, play and sleep before he faces the night alone.

It's a good idea to take someone with you when you go to collect your Cavalier puppy, so that one of you can drive and the other one can comfort the pup. An old towel to mop up any accidents is a good idea. When you collect him, make sure that you find out when he will need his next worming treatment and what vaccinations he has had. You should also receive a copy of your puppy's pedigree.

Although it is a very exciting time when you bring your Cavalier home for the first time, you should try to keep the atmosphere as calm and reassuring as possible. Moving to his new home is a complete change for your puppy

ABOVE: *A puppy will be ready for you to collect when he is about eight weeks of age.*

and he has to fit into a completely new environment. If there are other animals in your home you should always supervise the puppy until they have settled down together. Alternatively, if you are bringing an older dog into your home, he may already have insecurities that you will need to dispel.

LIFE CHANGES

Your puppy will have a lot of things to adjust to. At first, he may well feel lonely without his litter mates around him. A hot water bottle wrapped up in a blanket and a cuddly toy may help. Beware of going to your puppy if he cries during his first night with you. This is giving him the message that you will come running whenever he cries. You may also be tempted to take a miserable puppy into your own bed which you may not want to do in the long-term. A half-way house is to allow the puppy to sleep in a high-sided box in your room so that you can comfort any crying. The box will mean that he has to stay put and can't get into difficulties or fall down the stairs. After a couple of days, you can move the puppy into the kitchen.

If you are re-homing an older dog, be sure to call him by the name he is used to. Trying to change it to something you prefer will confuse and upset him.

LEFT: *If your puppy already has a name it recognizes, it will be confused if you change it.*

Cavalier Characteristics

Being a toy breed, Cavaliers are fairly small in size, weighing up to around 8.2 kilos (18 pounds) and between 30.5 to 33 centimetres (12 to 13 inches) high at the shoulder. The main physical appeal of the breed lies in its soulful eyes and lovely coat as well as its graceful and active mien. Although this coat will need looking after regularly it will only require bathing and brushing as no trimming, plucking or colouring is allowed. The Cavalier's sweet and melting expression and luminous dark brown eyes are also important breed characteristics.

CAVALIER COLOURS
Cavaliers come in four different colour combinations, and each has its adherents. The four colour ways are Blenheim, tricolour, ruby and black and tans.

Blenheim Cavaliers are the most numerous and the type even has its own shows. A Blenheim Cavalier will have rich chestnut markings on a pearly white ground. A show dog must have chestnut ears and the markings should be mostly symmetrical on the head, surrounding both eyes. The dogs should have a white blaze between the eyes and ears with the Blenheim spot of lozenge in the centre, on top of the head. Un-symmetrical markings or a

missing Blenheim spot are undesirable, as is excessive freckling on the facial hair. The chestnut marks will darken as your dog grows up.

Tricolour Cavaliers have jet black and tan markings on a pearly white background. The ears and the area around the eyes must be black while the eyebrows, cheeks, inside the ears, the top of the legs and the hair under the tail should be tan. Some tricolours also have the lozenge marking. Of course, not all tricolours have perfect markings for showing, but these dogs would make perfect pets. In tricolour puppies, the tan markings will be light but will darken with age.

Ruby Cavaliers have rich ruby-red hair all over, and are referred to as whole-coloured dogs. Dogs with even tiny patches of white hair are not suitable as show dogs, but make lovely pets. Your dog's ruby colour will darken as he grows up.

Black and Tan Cavaliers are quite unusual and difficult to source. They are jet black with tan eyebrows, cheeks and inner ears and tan markings on the chest, legs, and under the tail. Any white markings would mean that a dog could not be shown. The tan markings will darken with age.

ABOVE: *The tricolour Cavalier has black markings on a white background with chestnut on the eyebrows and cheeks.*

ABOVE: *The ruby Cavalier has a rich, solid chestnut coat.*

ABOVE: *A Blenheim Cavalier and top, black and tan Cavalier.*

3 CARING FOR YOUR CAVALIER

INOCULATIONS

One of the first and most important things you need to do for your Cavalier puppy is to make sure that he is enrolled into a comprehensive vaccination programme. This will protect him against the serious illnesses of distemper, hepatitis, parvovirus, leptospirosis, and kennel cough. He will need regular boosters throughout his life. You should keep your puppy at home until he is fully protected.

Puppies should be vaccinated at 6-9 weeks of age and then again at 10-12 weeks. They will usually become fully protected two weeks after the second vaccination but your vet may recommend a third dose for some puppies. The vaccine your vet will use will contain a modified dose of the disease that will stimulate your dog's immune system to produce antibodies that will be able to fight the disease. If your puppy is unwell, it may be a good idea to postpone his injections for a while, to minimise the small risk of adverse reaction. Most vaccines are injected into the scruff, but the kennel cough vaccine is given as drops into the nose. The kennel cough vaccine is usually only given to dogs that will be

left in boarding kennels, but it may also be useful if your dog needs to go into hospital for any reason.

When you take your unvaccinated puppy to the vet, you should make sure that you carry him and do not put him down in the surgery. If you plan to put your dog into a boarding kennel, you will need to keep an up-to-date card showing the vaccinations he has had.

Puppy Nutrition

As your puppy only has a small tummy, you will need to divide his food into several small meals. Four meals are usually considered best for puppies up to the age of twelve weeks old; breakfast, lunch, tea, and supper. Serving small meals at 7 a.m., 11 a.m., 3 p.m., and 6 or 7 p.m. works quite well. Don't allow your puppy Cavalier to go without food for more than six hours in the day. Leave his food down for around ten minutes so that he learns to eat up reasonably quickly. Don't worry if he doesn't finish his food at this age,

LEFT: *When your Cavalier reaches one year of age he can move to one meal a day.*

he may just be full. Dried food will swell in the puppy's tummy and he will soon feel satisfied. Leaving his food down for him to graze on is not very salubrious. At this age, intervals of three to four hours between his meals should be about right. Once your puppy is three months old, he can move to three meals a day. By the time he is six months old, two daily meals will be sufficient. When your dog reaches his first birthday, you can move to a single daily meal if you like, but many people prefer to divide their dog's food into two meals a day. If you are unhappy feeding a complete dry diet, you can always supplement this with some tasty treats.

Most Cavaliers have great appetites, and crave tidbits. You shouldn't struggle to get your puppy eating heartily. But other Cavalier puppies seem quite uninterested in food and you may worry that he's not getting enough. It may well help if you hand feed your puppy for a while, as Cavaliers will often take food from your hand that they would ignore in their bowls. They undoubtedly love the extra attention this brings. Although modern complete diets are extremely convenient, and contain everything your puppy needs, some owners prefer a more traditional puppy

diet of various nutritious foods. You should not rely on a diet of household scraps as it is very unlikely that this will provide enough nutrition for your puppy to grow up strong and healthy. If you decide to feed a traditional meat and biscuit diet rather than a complete food, you should be sure to give your dog a vitamin and mineral supplement each day.

Many Cavaliers put on a little

weight as they age. As this puts extra strain on their hearts, this should be prevented if at all possible. Swapping some of his food for cooked green vegetables or changing to a lower calorie version of his usual food should help. You should never give your dog human treats as these can also damage his teeth. Stick to dog treats and dog biscuits.

RIBHT: *Don't make the mistake of giving human treats to your dog.*

Puppy Exercise

Your new Cavalier puppy needs to be kept both mentally and physically active to make sure he is stimulated and happy. But he should not be taken out in public until at least two weeks after his final vaccination. Playing in the garden will be fine at this stage. But it is very important to exercise your Cavalier puppy in moderation as his bones are still soft and growing. Over-exercising a puppy can lead to damage and he will also tire quickly. Most experts recommend that Cavaliers should not be taken on long walks until they are around a year old.

As your Cavalier matures, exercise will become an increasingly important part of his day. Although he will appreciate long walks, he will also appreciate variety and having a free run. You can also take toys with you on his walk, so that you can play with these as you go.

PUPPY TOYS

Because Cavaliers like to chew it is important to make sure that anything you give your puppy has been tested for its resilience. Pull toys might spoil his teeth, so these may be best avoided. Squeaky toys should have the squeaker removed in case this gets swallowed. Small balls are also dangerous. Large balls and chew toys made out of tough rubber are best and homemade toys such as cardboard boxes will give your puppy hours of harmless fun.

WORMING

All dogs have worms at some point in their lives, and puppies are at the most risk from infestation. Worms are passed from the mother even before birth and through their milk. They then live in the puppy's intestine and feed on partly digested food. Untreated worms can cause serious illnesses in puppies, including weight loss, vomiting, diarrhoea, a swollen tummy and even death. An infested puppy cannot get the benefit from his food and will not thrive. He may also cough and his coat may look dull. Puppies need regular worming to combat this and should be

ABOVE: *A puppy will enjoy a free run.*

ABOVE: *It is safer to remove the squeak from a puppy toy.*

wormed from two weeks of age at two weekly intervals until they are twelve weeks of age, then every month until they are six months of age. Worming should continue at least three times a year with a recommended veterinary preparation for the rest of the dog's life.

Dogs are prone to two main types of worms, tapeworms and roundworms. Roundworms can appear like elastic bands, up to several inches in length. Tapeworms can appear like white grains of rice, which are joined together to form a tape. These are most commonly found in adult dogs and very rarely in puppies.

Your breeder should tell you about the worming programme they have been using and when the next treatment is due. It may be a good plan to let your puppy settle down before you worm him again. Twelve weeks is

usually considered to be a good age for this. Your vet can recommend a good product to use. Roundworms are spread through the environment while tapeworms are commonly spread by fleas, so it is wise to treat an infested dog with a flea treatment. Climate change has meant that dogs are now subject to new types of worm, Angiostrongylus, for example. These worms can live in the lungs or in the major blood vessels and may even cause death. Ordinary worming medicine does not work against these parasites. You should check with your vet to see which worms are problematic locally.

One of the first things to do with your new Cavalier puppy is to get him used to being handled, particularly so that you can do essential things such as clean his teeth and cut his nails.

Personal Care for Your Cavalier

TEETH CLEANING

A Cavalier will usually get his adult teeth at around the age of four-and-a-half months. You need to check which puppy teeth are loose and which have fallen out, and to see how the new ones are coming on. Gently lift the lips to check the teeth. Be especially careful if your puppy is teething. It is good to get your puppy used to this procedure so that both you and your vet will be able to examine his mouth without too much trouble. You should check the tongue to make sure that it looks normal, and check the dog's teeth and gums. The teeth should be clean and free from tartar.

If tartar builds up on the teeth his breath will smell, the teeth will become discoloured and eventually the gums will be affected, leading to infection.

Unfortunately, the ph value of your Cavalier's saliva will encourage the build-up of tartar. You can clean your dog's teeth with a special canine toothbrush, or a small piece of gauze wrapped around your finger. You can get special dog toothpaste from your vet (or on-line). This comes in various tasty flavours, such as chicken. Alternatively, you can use a paste of baking soda and water. Don't use fluoride toothpaste on puppies under the age of six months, as this can

ABOVE: *You can get special meat-flavoured toothpaste from your vet.*

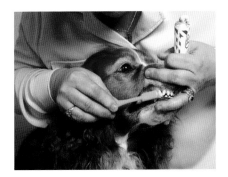

ABOVE: *Don't be tempted to used the toothpaste marketed for people as it will give your pup an upset tummy.*

ABOVE: *When your puppy gets used to this, it will be easier should a vet need to examine his mouth.*

interfere with the formation of his dental enamel. Human toothpaste should also be avoided as this can upset your dog's stomach.

Teeth cleaning chews and rawhide toys can help keep the tartar build up down.

ABOVE: *Most dogs dislike having their feet handled, so you should try to get your puppy used to this from an early age.*

ABOVE: *Clipping one paw at a time with other activities in between will be easier than attempting all four feet at once.*

EYE CARE

Your Cavalier's eyes should always be bright and clear and free from any foreign objects. You need to check your dog's eyes regularly as eye problems can be indicative of other health problems. You should watch out for excessive crustiness, tearing, red or white eyelid linings, tear-stained hair, closed eyes, cloudiness, a visible third eyelid, or unequal pupil size. If you see of these eye symptoms, you should contact your vet immediately.

NAIL CLIPPING

Unless your Cavalier spends a lot of time walking on hard surfaces that will help to keep his claws short, his nails will need regular clipping. If you hear them clicking on a hard surface,

it's time for a trim. Most dogs dislike having their feet handled, so you should try to get your puppy used to this from an early age. A dog's claw is made up of the nail itself, and the quick, which provides the blood supply to the nail. Avoid cutting into the quick as it will bleed profusely and is very sensitive. Don't worry if you can't do all your dog's nails in one session, it might be best to clip one paw at a time, with other activities in between.

nail-clippers

RIGHT: *Start your grooming session by using the hound glove to remove all the dead hair from his coat.*

steel comb

ABOVE: *You can remove tangles with a comb.*

GROOMING

All Cavaliers will require some degree of grooming to keep this coat in good condition. This needs to be done to ensure your dog's good health and maintain his appearance. It is worth investing in a small set of good quality grooming equipment. This should include:

- A steel comb.

- A soft bristle brush or wire hound glove with a fabric back (for polishing the coat).

- A hard bristle brush.

- Nail clippers.

- A pair of scissors

- Tissues

- A piece of chamois leather or silk

ABOVE: *It will help if your dog enjoys the grooming session.*

hard-bristled brush

RIGHT: *The coat should be brushed regularly to keep the silky coat at its best.*

GROOMING

Adult Cavaliers have well feathered ears and profuse silky hair on their chest, legs and tummy. This hair needs to be regularly groomed and kept clean and free from knots.

The sooner you start to groom your Cavalier puppy, the sooner he will get used to this kind of handling. This is vital if you want to show your dog. A Cavalier will usually have his adult coat by the time he is ten months old. Most dogs really enjoy the care and attention they receive while they are being groomed. The best way to start is to stand your dog on a firm surface that won't wobble. A table or work top is ideal. Start your grooming session

LEFT: *Take great care when handling the ears. These can be trimmed inside and out.*

ABOVE: *If your dog rolls in something smelly you will probably want to wash him.*

by using the hound glove or a brush to remove all the dead hair and foreign objects from his coat. The comb will come in handy when you are tidying the feathers on his legs and ears. Be as gentle as you can during this process. You should also groom inside and outside his ears, being very gentle and careful not to scratch the delicate skin in this area. Once you have finished brushing him, it is a good idea to wipe around his eyes with a damp tissue. Once he has his longer adult coat, you can buff this to a shine with the chamois or a piece of silk.

If the hair under your Cavalier's paws becomes dirty and matted, you can trim this with a pair of straight edged scissors.

A well-groomed dog does not need regular bathing. This tends to strip the natural oils from his coat. But if your Cavalier has rolled in something horrid, you probably won't feel you have a choice. A squirt of tomato sauce applied to the dirty area and then washed out will get rid of any dreadful smells. When washing your Cavalier, you should use a canine shampoo and make sure that this doesn't wash into his eyes. Use lukewarm water to wash the dog, and make sure that you thoroughly rinse the soap out of his hair. Once you have towelled him dry (or dried him with a hand-held hairdryer) you should brush out his coat.

Unwanted Visitors

Unfortunately, a Cavalier's luxurious coat seems to be the ideal home for several parasites including fleas, lice, ticks, ear mites and harvest mites.

FLEAS

Fleas are small, flat, wingless, blood-sucking insects that are an irritation to dogs and their owners alike. They can also can carry and transmit serious diseases and other parasites (such as tapeworms). They are also the leading cause of skin problems in domestic dogs. Although they can't fly, fleas have powerful rear legs and can jump to extraordinary lengths. There are many types of flea, all of which reproduce rapidly and profusely. Despite its name, the ordinary cat flea is by far the most common flea that bothers pet dogs. Dogs become infested if good flea prevention isn't followed. Dogs can also get fleas by having contact with other animals that have a flea problem.

ABOVE: *Unfortunately, a Cavalier's luxurious coat seems to be the ideal home for several parasites.*

ABOVE: *Make sure you wash the bedding regularly to discourage parasites.*

Fortunately, there are many things that dog owners can do to keep fleas under control. Most dogs that have fleas will find them irritating and will scratch, but some can have a severe reaction to flea bites (flea dermatitis). If you think that you have found flea debris in your dog's coat, collect some of the black grit from the coat and put it on a white tissue. If the black grit goes blood-coloured when you dampen it, your dog has fleas. Wash the dog as quickly as possible, not forgetting his bedding and around the house. There are many excellent flea-control preparations on the market today, but your vet will probably be able to sell you the most effective.

TICKS

Ticks can sometimes be found in your dog's coat in the summer months. Ticks are parasites of sheep and cattle. The adult tick starts life small and spider-like. It crawls over the body, finds a suitable place and bites into the skin. It will stay in this position for about two weeks until fully engorged with blood, swollen to the size of a pea and beige in colour. The tick will then drop off the host and, if female, lay eggs in the grass. These hatch into larvae which will then find a host. After a feed, these larvae drop off, undergo change and find another host. It takes three larvae changes, each taking a year, before the adult form is arrived at and the cycle is then repeated. Ticks can be removed by using flea-control remedies, some of which are also designed to remove ticks. Other methods involve removing the tick with special forceps, making sure you grasp the head. This is made easier by killing the tick first. If you don't manage to remove the tick's mouth parts, the bite can become infected.

LICE

Lice are grey, about 2mm long and they lay small eggs (nits) which stick to the dog's hair and can look like scurf. Dogs can then scratch and create bald patches. You should give your dog repeat treatments of insecticide sprays or baths to kill the adults and any hatching larvae. They often appear in a Cavalier's ears.

HARVEST MITES

Harvest mites infestation occurs in the late summer, starting around late July. They are little orange mites which affect the feet, legs and skin of the tummy and can cause immense irritation. The orange mite can just be seen with a naked eye. Treat with benzyl benzoate, a white emulsion which can be bought at the chemist, which should be rubbed into the affected parts. Many of the flea insecticides will also treat this complaint.

EAR MITES

A Cavalier's heavy ear flaps can stop a good circulation of air around his ears. Waxy deposits in this area may mean that he had ear mites, especially if he is scratching. Ear drops can get rid of them and regular application should keep them away.

The Veteran Cavalier

A Cavalier has an average life expectancy of between ten and twelve years, but individual dogs can live up to the age of fifteen. Birth to two years old is usually considered to be the growth stage, two years to five years old the young adult stage, five to eight years middle age, and eight years plus old age. Of course, as any dog gets older he may well need more day-to-day care and veterinary treatment.

ABOVE: *Dogs can live to the age of fifteen years.*

To many owners their veteran Cavalier becomes more precious as he ages. He will have given the best years of his life to be your companion. There are still some lovely times that you can have together as Cavaliers can live to a good age.

As your dog ages his needs will change and the way you care for him will need to keep up with this. Good sense will tell you how much exercise he wants. A dog over the age of eight should be taken for shorter walks at his old pace. Of course, each dog will age at his own rate, so discretion and discernment is required.

Diet is perhaps one of the important changes you will notice as your dog ages. He will no longer require as much food. Teeth may not be as good as they were, so an entirely hard diet may no longer be suitable. It might also suit your older dog to eat two smaller meals each day so that his digestive system can cope better. Many dog food manufacturers offer diets that have been specially designed for the older dog. These may well be appropriate for your older Cavalier.

If your dog is taking less exercise you may also find that you need to trim his nails more often, and you need to make absolutely sure that you

ABOVE: *Older dogs need to be kept comfortable and warm.*

keep his coat clean and comfortable. Grooming will also give you a chance to check him over and notice any health problems at an early stage.

Older Cavaliers should always be kept comfortable and warm. You should never allow your older dog to get cold and wet. Make sure his bed is somewhere where the temperature is constant and free of draughts. He will sleep longer and more soundly than when he was younger. If you have younger dogs in the family make sure the old dog is not left out but, at the same time, do not let the young dogs either annoy or disturb the old dog when he is sleeping. You should also protect the old dog from any over-boisterous activities from the younger dogs.

Although every day with your dog is precious, if your Cavalier is failing in health and losing his quality of life you may need to consider putting him to sleep. Your vet will help you make that decision when the time comes. It is the hardest decision to make but don't let your dog suffer at the end; you owe it to him to have a dignified and painless departure from the world.

4 TRAINING YOUR CAVALIER

Basic obedience is important for any dog, but Cavaliers are sweet and biddable and will want to please you. The first few weeks after you bring your puppy home are important in setting the tone of your future relationship. It will be completely unnecessary to smack your dog, or punish him in any way. A sharp tone of voice and a firm "No!" should be sufficient. He is young and although he will certainly make mistakes, he will never be naughty on purpose. If he makes mistakes, you need to forgive and correct him gently. As your puppy grows, it may be a good idea to enrol him in local obedience classes, but you can start his training the moment you bring him home to live with you.

HOUSE TRAINING

House training is the first sort of training that you should begin with your puppy. It should begin as soon as you first arrive home with him. With vigilance and positive training methods, most puppies quickly learn how to be clean in the house. Being a highly intelligent breed, Cavaliers are particularly quick to learn.

House training will be easier if your puppy has a settled routine, sleeping and eating at the same times during the day. Puppies usually need to relieve themselves when they wake up, during play, and after meals. You should also watch for signs indicating that your puppy wants to go to the toilet; restlessness, whining, tail raising, sniffing and circling around. You should take your puppy to the same place in the garden on each of these occasions. You should encourage him with a consistent phrase such as "toilet." As soon as the puppy performs you should praise him and play with him. You may be surprised how often your puppy needs to relieve himself, but remember he has only a small bladder at this age. This means that he will find it very difficult to stay clean all night long, so it may be a good idea to leave some newspaper down at night.

If your puppy makes a mistake you need to clean up as well as you can so that no smell lingers. any lingering odour might give the puppy the idea that he can use that spot for his "business" in the future. While some puppies are easier to house train than others, you should remember that your puppy will not have full bladder control until he is about four months old and should never be punished for making mistakes.

OPPOSITE: *The Cavalier is an intelligent and responsive dog which will make training easier.*

Name Training

The very first thing is to teach your puppy his name. You need to call him over to you with a treat in your hand, or be ready to play. You should sound excited and praise him lavishly when he comes to you. A small tidbit works well for Cavaliers! If you try to establish "coming when called" at an early age this will become second nature to him, and may save his life in a dangerous situation. It's a good idea to have imprinted this lesson on your dog before allowing him any free range exercise.

TEACHING RECALL

If you are struggling to get your puppy to come to you, try carrying a treat in a crinkly paper bag. If your puppy doesn't come when you call him you can rustle the bag while you repeat his name. As soon as he has made the connection between the rustling paper and the treat he will always come to

ABOVE: *The first thing to teach your puppy is to recognize his name.*

ABOVE: *Give a treat when the puppy comes when you call his name and he will soon learn to associate the two.*

you. When he does you should stroke and praise him.

If your Cavalier decides to disobey you use a low firm voice to get his attention. You don't need to shout! Once you have it you should immediately change your tone to a soft and encouraging tone and call him again. This should do the trick. When he has obeyed you give him a treat and praise him. You should also remember that however angry your dog has made you by refusing to come when he has been called, you must never punish him when he does finally come to you. This will confuse him and undermine his trust in your leadership.

A recall lead is useful for this exercise once you are ready to practise in an open space.

ABOVE: *Keep the training fun!.*

ABOVE: *Training lead.*

Training Tips

ABOVE: *Make sure you have your puppy's attention before you give a command.*

Before you move on to the next steps of training your puppy to sit, stay and walk to heel etc. there are some basic training tips that it are well worth remembering.

You should always make sure that you have your puppy's attention before you give a command. You should aim only to give commands that your puppy will obey, so you need to make sure that he is listening to you. You can do this by calling his name or snapping your fingers until you have good eye contact with him.

Then give your command and make sure that your puppy follows through. Give him time to respond but ensure that he does as you have asked. Don't keep repeating the command as this means that your pup chooses when he obeys you. The idea is that he should obey you at once.

Puppies have only a short attention span, so you should keep your training sessions to no more than five or ten minutes. Your puppy won't be able to focus for much longer than this. It's important to

54

keep the atmosphere of the training sessions as positive as possible, with lots of praise. If your puppy seems confused by a new command go back to something you know he can do so that you can end the session on a positive note. If you are using training treats as part of your method you may well find that it's better to time your sessions before meals, when the puppy might be a little hungry. But as your puppy gradually learns your commands you should phase out the treats, as you don't want to have to rely on treats in the long term.

In training your dog you should try to step into the role of being a positive pack leader or parent to your dog. Bonding with your dog in his early life and encouraging him to mix with other people and animals will help him to be calm and confident when he grows up. Because he will not be protected by his vaccinations in these early weeks you will need to carry him if he goes outside your house and garden. Your attitude is very crucial at this stage in his life. If he has your calm and unqualified support, it will help him to develop into the kind of well socialised dog that will be easy to train.

RIGHT: *As you start to train the dog you are stepping into the role of his pack leader.*

Lead Training

Most Cavaliers learn how to walk on the lead quite quickly. Their natural inclination is to keep close to you so attaching a lead to your pup's collar is usually no problem. Twelve to fourteen weeks is a good age for a puppy to start wearing his first collar. The puppy's neck will be very soft and delicate so you should use a very soft and comfortable collar. Your puppy will soon grow out of this, so wait until he is at least six months of age before you buy him anything expensive.

The best place to begin training your puppy is in your garden. In this safe and controlled environment your puppy can learn about walking on the lead where there is nothing to upset or distract him. Encourage him and praise him as he walks well, but do not allow him to rush forwards and pull. If he does, keep calm and talk to him, then persuade him to walk a few steps and praise again. It will not take long for him to learn. Calm lead work will build a strong bond of trust between you so that when he goes out into the world and meets new and scary things he will look to you for reassurance. You have several weeks to work on this exercise before his vaccinations are complete and he can go into the outside world.

Training To Heel

The art of training your Cavalier to "heel" is a simple extension of training your puppy to work on the lead. The greater control the exercise gives you over your puppy is particularly important in an urban environment. A head collar or anti-pull harness can be helpful during heelwork training. The object of the exercise is to have the puppy walking by your side with his head level with your left leg.

Start the exercise with your dog close to your left leg, with both of you facing the same way. Have one of your pup's favourite treats in your left hand. Hold the treat up near your waist, not directly in front of your dog's nose. Now say your dog's name to get his attention and to gain eye contact. Immediately take two steps forward and then stop. If your dog moves with you and is still in the heel position enthusiastically praise him and give a treat.

As soon as your puppy swallows his reward repeat the heeling process again. Say his name and take two steps forward while saying "come on" or "that's a good boy." Then stop, praise your dog and give him a treat. Only ever give the reward when your dog is still in the heel position. It's important to remember that you are using the treat to reward good behaviour rather than to lure or bribe him.

If at any time your dog lags behind or forges ahead of you, hold off with your praise and rewards. Simply start the exercise again.

Teaching the Sit

ABOVE: *When your puppy has learnt to site you can progress to the stay command.*

Teaching your puppy to sit is a useful exercise, as it shows him that you are in control. It can also calm a difficult situation. Most Cavaliers will sit naturally just by voice. If, however, your puppy does not understand repeat the command "sit" and gently push the puppy's hindquarters down into the sitting position and then reward with a treat. The puppy will learn quickly.

TEACHING THE DOWN

The Down is the next command after Sit. Start with your puppy at the Sit position. Have a treat in your hand which you then hold on the floor in front of the puppy. When the puppy goes down for it give the command "Down" followed by the reward and praise. When this exercise is repeated several times the puppy will go down without you having to put your hand to the floor, but reward and praise every time until it is firmly established. If the puppy will not go down at the start of this training you can give very gentle pressure on the forequarters to encourage him to go down to the floor.

TEACHING THE STAY

Learning to "Stay" is important to all dogs. When you first start to teach your puppy to stay it is best to have him on the lead. Ask the puppy to either sit, or go down, with the lead extended from you to the puppy; walk away backwards (facing the puppy) and repeat the command "Stay". When you get as far as the end of the lead, stand still for a few seconds, ask the puppy to come, and praise him. Gradually lengthen the distance you leave the puppy and always give praise when

he does it right. If the puppy breaks the Stay take him back to where you left him at Sit or Down and repeat the exercise, but do not go so far away from him before you call him. This exercise will take time and patience; little and often is best. It may be helpful if you use a hand signal as well as the command.

ABOVE: *Teach the down position and reward with a treat.*

ABOVE: *Stay can be used with the down position and you can gradually increase the distance.* **59**

5 CAVALIER SPORTS

Cavaliers take part in several different kinds of canine competitions, including mini-agility, Flyball, tracking and obedience.

COMPETITIVE OBEDIENCE
Many Cavaliers take part in competitive obedience trials at dog shows around the world. This rewarding sport is the logical extension of good training. Each level of obedience trial has a set list of exercises and requirements for dogs and their handlers to follow as closely as possible. Marks are awarded for the ability of the combined dog/handler team. As well as taking your dog's training to a higher level, competitive obedience can be highly enjoyable for both dogs and humans and a great bonding experience.

MINI-AGILITY
Cavaliers are naturally suited to agility competitions. They want to work with their handlers and obey their instructions. Their small size gives them an advantage over bigger dogs on obstacles such as the tunnels, dog walk and see-saw. You shouldn't allow your Cavalier to attempt an agility course until he is fully grown, or at least a year old. Mini-agility is a scaled down version of agility designed for smaller dogs like the Cavalier.

Competitive agility and mini-agility date back to the Crufts dog shows of the late 1970s. To entertain the audience in the interval dogs ran around a specially designed course against the clock. The inspiration behind the concept was competitive horse jumping. The sport quickly spread to the United States and has now spread around the world. The sport consists of a dog and handler running around an obstacle course together. The obstacles are usually all different, but may include a variety of hurdles, an A-frame, a dog-walk, a see-saw, a tunnel, a long jump and a tyre. The competing dog/handler teams are scored for speed and accuracy. The dogs participate off the lead and it is not permissible to encourage them with food or toys. The handler can only use voice and hand signals to instruct their dog.

FLYBALL
Cavaliers can also make great Flyball competitors. They love to play and this is a great opportunity for young and fit dogs to play and socialise. As well as keeping Cavaliers and their owners fit, competing in Flyball can help to build the rapport between dog and owner.

Flyball is a modern variant of canine agility that has become very popular

ABOVE: *Cavaliers are naturally suited to agility competitions.*

in recent years. Essentially, Flyball is a sport in which teams of four dogs run in relays over a line of hurdles to a box where the dogs collect a tennis ball that they then return to their handlers. In Britain it is governed by the British Flyball Association and in America the sport is regulated by the North American Flyball Association.

TRACKING

Cavaliers retain enough of their sporting heritage to enable them to be very good tracking dogs. In tracking competitions, a dog follows a scent trail laid by someone walking over the ground. The dog must keep closely to the original track. He may get some help from air scent, but to succeed the dog must keep its head close to the ground. As the handler doesn't know where the track has been laid, he must learn to trust his Cavalier and be able to read his body language.

Therapy Cavaliers

ABOVE: *The gentle Cavalier makes a perfect therapy dog.*

Cavaliers are so friendly and affectionate that they make wonderful therapy dogs. Cavaliers were originally bred to be comfort and companion dogs, and cuddling Cavaliers was even prescribed by early doctors. Therapy dogs are usually trained from puppies to be "bombproof" by being exposed to lots of different situations, people and noises. Therapy dogs work with all kinds of different people, including the elderly, disabled and sick. Their loving and kind natures are ideal for this kind of important work and contact with these lovely dogs can be very healing and beneficial.

6 SHOWING YOUR CAVALIER KING CHARLES SPANIEL

If you bought your Cavalier puppy from a line of show dogs, you may wish to show him. This will mean that your dog will be compared to the Cavalier breed standard. This lays down the ideal character, temperament and appearance for the breed by which your dog will be judged.

The first thing that any good judge will be looking for is a sound and healthy dog that is a good example of the breed. No reputable breeder would allow an unhealthy dog, or a dog with health issues to produce a litter.

A good Cavalier should be an active, graceful, and well-balanced dog. He should be gay and free in his movements. Cavaliers are brave and sporting by nature but also gentle and affectionate.

In temperament, a good Cavalier should be demonstrably extrovert, friendly, happy and biddable. Any sign of bad temper or aggression is totally out of character for this breed. His general appearance should be merry and active, with a friendly wagging tail.

In size, he should be 30.5 to 33 centimetres (12 to 13 inches) high at the withers, and between 5.8 and 8.2 kilos (13 and 18 pounds) in weight.

BELOW: *The judge will look for a sound, healthy dog with no aggression.*

63

Cavalier Breed Standard

THE HEAD
A Cavalier's head should be slightly rounded, but without a dome or peak. Its appearance should be flat because of the high placement of the ears.

THE EYES
The Cavalier's eyes are the essence of the dog's appeal, with their lustrous and limpid look and clever and trusting expression. They should be very dark brown and have a slight cushioning under the eyes that contribute to their sweet and gentle expression.

THE EARS
A Cavalier's ears should be set high, but not close, on top of the head. The ear leathers should be long with silky feathering. When the dog is alert the ears should fan slightly forward to frame the face.

THE MUZZLE
The Cavalier's muzzle should be well tapered and his mouth level. No bare flesh should show through the hair on the muzzle. The teeth should be strong and clean and the upper teeth should

LEFT: *The Cavalier's eyes are lustrous and limpid.*

overlap the lower ones in a close scissor bite. The nose should have a shallow stop and should measure at least 3.8 centimetres (1.5 inches) from base to tip. The nostrils should be completely black.

THE BODY
The body should be short-coupled, strong and compact with a deep and well developed chest that leaves ample heart room. The ribs should be well sprung but not barrelled. The neck should be fairly long, but not throaty. It should be well muscled and set into nicely sloping shoulders. These should be moderately angular. The Cavalier's back should be level and lead into

strong and well muscled hind quarters. Viewed from the rear, the hind legs should be parallel from hock to heel. The Forelegs should be straight and set well under the dog, so that the elbows are held close to his sides.

THE TAIL
A Cavalier should carry his tail level with his back. It should be merry and in constant motion when the dog is in action. In Britain, Cavaliers are not docked. In America the last third of the tail is sometimes docked.

TESTICLES
A male Cavalier should have two testicles fully descended into the scrotum.

THE COAT
A Cavalier's coat should be long and silky and very soft to the touch. It should not be curly but may have a slight wave. The feathering on the ears, legs and tail should be long. The feet should also be feathered. It is not permissible to trim your Cavalier's hair, but the hair under the feet and between the pads may be tidied up.

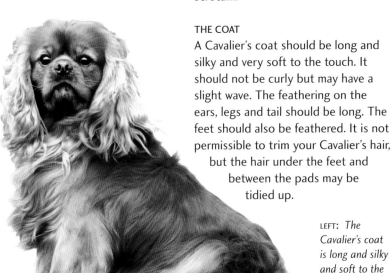

LEFT: *The Cavalier's coat is long and silky and soft to the touch.*

Dog Shows

ABOVE: *Dog shows may involve a lot of work but can be great fun for the owner and the dog.*

Showing your dog can be a great way to make new friends and can be a highly absorbing hobby. There are all kinds of dog shows from the informal to the highly competitive and there are also parallel events for young dog handlers. So long as you approach dog shows with good sportsmanship and a sense of humour they can be great fun. You will need a small amount of equipment to show your dog. This should include a good grooming kit, a show lead, and a water bowl. You may

find it safe and convenient to take your dog to shows in a dog crate. At the show itself the judge will want to check your dog over and see him in action moving around the show ring. In Britain all dog shows are regulated by the Kennel Club.

Before you show your own dog it is a very good idea to attend a dog show and see what will be expected of you and your Cavalier. This may give you an idea of how the dogs are prepared for showing. Bathing a day or so before the show should keep the coat smart and pearly white. He will then need a thorough grooming, especially around the feathers.

ENTERING A SHOW

Most dog shows ask their participants to fill in a set of entry forms. You need to fill in these show entry forms very carefully, as mistakes may mean disqualification. In the UK your dog also needs to be Kennel Club-registered in your name before you can show him. Novice owners may think that if a dog has been registered by the breeder he can be shown. But this is not the case. Make sure that you arrive at the show in good time so that you and your Cavalier can settle down in the busy atmosphere and relax.

IN THE RING

All dog show judges have their own system of judging, but most judges will ask participants to line up as a class. The judge will then ask you all to move together before inspecting the dogs individually. They will then ask you to move your dog on his own so that he can give him a full inspection. Most judges start their examination at the dog's head. This will include

looking at your Cavalier's mouth to see if he has the breed's correct bite. The judge will feel the body, forequarters and hindquarters. He will also check your dog's paws, pads and his tail. The judge, with both hands, will span the dog behind the shoulders and lift him briefly to assess his weight.

The judge will then ask you to move the dog around the ring. He might ask you to move up and down, or in a triangle. This is so that he can assess the dog's movement from the front and rear and in profile. When the judge has reached a decision, he will place the dogs in order of merit. Don't take it too badly if you don't win on this occasion, you and your Cavalier may be more lucky next time you venture into the show ring.

LEFT: *A judge will will check the dog's mouth to see if the bite is correct.*

7 BREEDING CAVALIERS

Breeding a litter of puppies can be very rewarding, but it can also be costly and time consuming. Each pregnancy will also put your bitch at risk, so you need to consider the pros and cons very carefully. You should not breed from your bitch if she has any health issues or faults that she would perpetuate in her puppies. With Cavaliers, the most important illnesses to avoid are early hearing trouble, slipping patellas and hernias. You will want to make every effort to ensure that the puppies that you breed have sound temperaments, are healthy and are good examples of the breed. You will also want to make absolutely sure that your puppies go to good homes.

Before you go ahead and breed your litter, you would be well advised to ask yourself some serious questions. Do you have the time to look after your litter until they go to their new homes (around eight weeks)? Are you knowledgeable enough to advise your puppies' new owners about the various aspects of caring for their puppies, including their diet, training and health problems? Can you afford the veterinary bills for your bitch's ante-natal care and for her litter? Do you know enough to help the bitch during her labour? Could you afford for your bitch to have a caesarean section if

she needs one? Are you equipped to raise the puppies with everything they need including worming, vaccinations and socialisation? Most importantly of all perhaps, will you be able to place your pups into good homes and would you have the resources to take puppies back if the homes you sold them to prove unsuitable?

Many people breed from their Cavalier bitch because they would like to keep a puppy for themselves and most bitches sail through whelping and very much enjoy having puppies. You should not breed from your Cavalier until at least the third time she comes in season, at approximately eighteen months old and ideally before she is three years old. Her final litter should be born before she is eight years old.

THE STUD DOG

The demands on dog breeders grow increasingly complex to ensure that future generations of dogs are bred responsibly. The over-riding consideration is the health of any potential puppies. This is particularly important when you are looking for a stud dog. He must have a good temperament, good health and be a good example of the Cavalier King Charles Spaniel. If your bitch came from a reputable breeder, go back

RIGHT: *You should take the time to visit the intended stud dog.*

to them and ask their advice about what stud dog to use. It is always best to use a proven, experienced stud dog. Predicting breed type and characteristics requires experience. If you are new to dog breeding then you should seriously consider joining an appropriate breed club where you will be able to meet and talk to some very experienced breeders.

You should certainly take the time to go and see the dog that may become the father of your puppies. You should also show your bitch's pedigree to the owner of the stud dog so that they can approve of her. Ask what the stud fee is and what conditions will be included; for example, do you get at least two matings if necessary and if your bitch fails to have puppies, does the stud

fee cover a free return? Most stud dog owners offer this. You then need to work out when your bitch will be in season and when the puppies will be born.

There is a lot of time and work with puppies, so make sure you are going to be able to give it when they are born.

MATING

New breeders need to concentrate on finding out when their bitch comes into season. If you don't realise until your bitch has been in season for several days, it may be too late. This is disappointing if all the plans have been made. You will need to check your bitch virtually every day for the start of her season. The first sign is the vulva swelling. Some bitches' vulvas swell and do not show any signs of red

69

discharge, others will show very little red discharge. Count from the day her vulva becomes swollen, just in case she is a bitch that has clear seasons.

Once your bitch is showing colour wait until the discharge becomes paler until you take her to be mated. You can check this by using either a white tissue to dab the vulva morning and night to determine the colour change, or you can put a white cover on her bedding so that you can monitor the colour change. If your bitch does not show any colour change you will need to count the days after she comes into season; ten to twelve days after coming in season is probably the best guide. However, some bitches are ready to mate after just six days into their season and have produced puppies from this mating, but this does not happen very often.

Once the bitch has been mated, you must keep her away from other male dogs until she is completely out of season. It would probably be wise to keep her away from any male dog all the time she

is in season.

First-time breeders can also be nervous. Not everyone is aware that mating dogs "tie" or "lock" together during mating, on average usually for about twenty to thirty minutes. Sometimes dogs are locked together for hours, although this is very rare. It is usual to have your bitch mated twice, approximately forty-eight hours apart; once this is done take your bitch home and keep her secure and quiet.

Occasionally a bitch will, after being mated, have a red discharge from her vulva, even as late as three to four weeks after mating. This usually indicates that the bitch is in whelp and there is activity within the womb. In the early days of pregnancy nothing should be changed, so treat her normally.

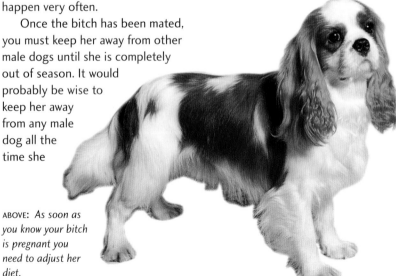

ABOVE: *As soon as you know your bitch is pregnant you need to adjust her diet.*

Pregnancy

A bitch is usually pregnant for sixty-three days or nine weeks, but you should be prepared for her to give birth up to five days early or four days late. You may be able to see that your bitch is pregnant from about five weeks, although some bitches do not show until seven weeks. Early signs of pregnancy are a thickening around the waist. Her vulva may remain slightly swollen and there may be a slight colourless discharge. She may also lose her appetite, and she may be sick. She may also become very quiet. On the other hand, she may show no signs at all but still could be pregnant. If you can see signs of her pregnancy very early, this may indicate that she is having a large litter.

As soon as you know that your bitch is pregnant you need to change her diet from approximately five weeks onwards. As the puppies grow bigger she will not be able to eat as much as she needs in just one feed. It is advisable to split her food into at least two meals a day, and up to four feeds a day towards the end of her pregnancy. It is very important to keep your bitch well nourished so that she will have the energy she needs to give birth. In the final two weeks, your bitch's exercise should be supervised so she is not overtired. Gentle exercise is good for

her but car journeys should probably be avoided. You should also stop your bitch jumping down from anything higher than two feet tall. Towards the end of the pregnancy your bitch will probably have a sticky clear discharge from her vulva; this is normal. Any other colour is not and may mean she could be aborting her puppies and needs to see the vet.

WHELPING

As your bitch's due date approaches you should decide where she will give birth. This needs to be somewhere comfortable, quiet and warm (around 21.1 degrees Centigrade or 70 degrees Fahrenheit). It would be sensible to inform your veterinary practice that your bitch is due to whelp. Then if you do need to consult them in the middle of the night they are better able to give you any help you need.

When your bitch goes into labour the best thing to do is to sit quietly near her and give her comfort and reassurance as and when she needs it. Her body temperature will drop from the normal temperature of 38.6 degrees Centigrade (101.5 degrees Fahrenheit) to 37.2 degrees Centigrade (99 degrees Fahrenheit). This stage of labour can last as long as twenty-four hours, and she may pant and tremble

and dig up her bedding and look totally distressed. Don't worry, this is quite normal. You should only offer her clean water at this stage, as many bitches vomit during labour. You may also wish to trim the long hair around her tummy and hindquarters to stop this getting in the way. Your bitch will then go into the next stage when strong contractions will start. She will start to push as they increase in intensity. Her first pushes will be light and get much stronger. Your bitch may also pass a water bag which will then break, producing a clear greenish liquid. Soon after this the contractions will get stronger and a puppy should be born within 20-30 minutes. This second

stage of labour can last between 3 and 24 hours with puppies being born within 20 minutes of each other, but there can be up to two hours between puppies. Mum will usually clean the puppy of its covering membrane and bite through the umbilical cord. Some puppies are born tail and hind feet first, but this isn't a problem. Each puppy should be followed by the afterbirth or placenta.

If your bitch is busy delivering the next puppy, you should remove the membrane from the puppy (so that he can breathe) and dry him with a clean facecloth. Rubbing will encourage him to take his first breath and crying helps to clear his airways. You should also tie a piece of heavy thread around the cord approximately one inch from the pup's body, then tie another knot a little further from the first and use clean scissors to cut the cord between the knots. Be very careful not to cut too close to the puppy, and dip the end of the cord in tincture of iodine or chlorhexidine.

The third stage of labour is the passing of the placentas. You should count them to make sure that none are retained in the uterus. Some bitches eat the placentas which contain nutrients that help her body to recover. If you are unsure how things are going, the bitch is straining, or a placenta

is retained, you should call your vet immediately. He can give your bitch an injection that will result in the bitch expelling the retained afterbirth.

When your bitch's labour is finished, you should get the mother something to eat and drink, and help her to go outside and relieve herself. Goats milk with honey or glucose dissolved in it will ensure that she has enough fluid on board to produce milk for the puppies.

You should remove and replace the soiled nest covers and then give the new family some time alone. Your bitch will probably want to sleep while she suckles the puppies. This first

ABOVE: *Your Cavalier may be a brilliant mother but if not, you will have to help out.*

73

milk is very important as it contains colostrum that contains the mother's antibodies and will protect them until they are old enough to be vaccinated. It may be wise for your vet to see the bitch and puppies soon after whelping. He can check the puppies for any abnormalities.

AFTER THE WHELPING

If your bitch isn't interested in taking care of her puppies and doesn't show any concern for them for more than an hour you may need to take over looking after them. You should also consult your vet for advice. Hand-rearing may be necessary, especially if the bitch doesn't seem able to produce any milk. Other bitches are fantastic mothers and don't even want to leave their puppies so that they can go to the toilet.

It is very important that your new mother eats well. After eating the rich afterbirths your bitch may refuse food for a while and may go off her food altogether. You need to tempt her with some tasty treats. It is often preferable to feed your bitch several small meals a day, consisting of really good quality food. She will also need to eat well to produce enough milk for her growing puppies.

ECLAMPSIA

Eclampsia is a life-threatening condition that results from the bitch's loss of calcium during pregnancy (making the puppy's bones) and in her milk. It usually happens within a few weeks of her giving birth. Small dogs

with large litters have an especially high risk of the condition. It can be avoided by a good diet in pregnancy. Symptoms of this frightening illness (which can start very quickly) include panting, drooling, vomiting, restlessness, muscle spasms, convulsions, breathing difficulties, heart problems and seizures. Eclampsia is a serious medical emergency and your dog will need urgent treatment, which will usually include calcium. This can be given intravenously. Once treated, your bitch should make a full and speedy recovery. However, the puppies should be fed for at least 24 or 36 hours. If there is any recurrence, she should not suckle the puppies again.

THE NEW LITTER
The new puppies will start to grow a day or so after they are born. They should put on a few ounces in weight each week. Their eyes should open within twelve or fifteen days. The first teeth appear at around twenty-eight days. Their pink noses will soon start to go black!

WEANING THE PUPPIES
You should start weaning the puppies between the age of two and three weeks. Worming is also one of the most important things at this time. Puppies can be born infected by worms and worms will prevent them from thriving. The puppies will need worming at two weeks of age. This can be done with

a liquid puppy wormer that your vet will supply. They should be wormed twice more before the age of eight weeks. As you start to wean your puppies, you can give them saucers of warmed puppy milk several times a day. When the puppies have accepted the puppy milk you can move on to solids. This could be canned puppy meat or dried food formulated for puppies. This should be fed warm. Dried food should be soaked until the puppies' teeth are stronger when it can be fed dry. Your puppies should also have constant access to fresh water. This is particularly important if you are feeding dried food as this can make the puppies very thirsty. By the age of eight weeks your puppies should be fully weaned and eating and drinking independently. They will then be ready for re-homing.

8 CAVALIER HEALTH CARE

Most Cavaliers enjoy long and healthy lives, but they do have some hereditary problems to look out for.

HIP DYSPLASIA

Is a serious condition that affects several breeds of dog, including Cavaliers. This degenerative condition affects the hip joint of the hind legs and can be crippling. A puppy can be born with seemingly normal hips, but the symptoms of the condition can appear as he matures. The condition can cause pain and lameness. It can be diagnosed by an X-ray.

ENTROPION

Entropion is a painful condition in which a dog's eyelids roll inward, allowing the eyelashes to rub against the cornea and irritate it. The upper and/or lower eyelids can be involved, and the condition can occur in either one eye or both. A dog with entropion will squint and have an excessive amount of tears coming from the affected eye. While any dog can have entropion, there is often a genetic factor. When caused by genetics, the condition will show up before a dog's first birthday.

Common Canine Ailments

ANAL GLANDS: A dog's anal glands are located on either side of the anus. Their original use was for scent marking. As a rule these glands are emptied by defecation but, if the dog's motions are soft and too loose, there is not the pressure on the glands which is needed to clear them. An affected dog will drag his rear end along the floor, or will attempt to chew or lick near his tail area in order to relieve the irritation caused by overfilled anal glands. An abscess may occur if they are not cleaned. If you are unable to empty them yourself, it would be advisable to get your vet to do it for the dog's comfort.

ARTHRTIS: This is a complaint that usually affects older dogs. A veteran Cavalier may endure stiffness, but do not allow the dog to suffer unnecessarily as there are several remedies that greatly benefit this complaint.

BURNS AND SCALDS: The treatment for burns and scalds is the same as for humans. Rinse the affected area under a cold tap or hosepipe in order to take the heat out; if necessary, cut away as much hair as possible. In minor cases apply a suitable soothing ointment; in serious cases your vet must be consulted. A badly burned dog will be suffering from shock and should be kept warm and quiet in his bed or box.

CONSTIPTATION: If this happens frequently it probably indicates incorrect feeding, so you may want to adjust your feeding regime. Gnawing bones can also cause this problem in some dogs. Changing your dog's exercise patterns can sometimes cause constipation. Dogs are creatures of habit and, if they have to wait too long to pass a motion, this can cause constipation. When a dog is constipated, occasionally it will pass a smearing of blood with the motion. As long as it is only a trace it will resolve itself but, if there is any considerable amount then it should be considered serious. Home remedies for an odd incident of constipation include a small amount of olive oil, mineral oil, or milk. You should also make sure that your dog is drinking enough as this in itself can cause constipation. If the attack lasts for longer than twenty-four hours or the dog seems to be straining excessively, you should consult your vet immediately as this may indicate a blockage.

DIARRHOEA: There can be many reasons for this condition. The dog's diet, a change of diet, or eating something nasty can start a bout of diarrhoea. This can usually be stopped by fasting the dog for twenty-four hours. You should give him a solution of glucose and water to drink so that he does not become dehydrated. Start feeding again with light, easy-to-digest foods such as chicken or fish. Diarrhoea can also be a sign of serious problems such as gastroenteritis, parvovirus, worm infestation, foreign bodies in the gut or internal organ problems. Stress can also trigger diarrhoea, just as it does in humans. You should monitor your dog closely while he suffers from diarrhoea, and if a bout turns into something more persistent you should take him to the vet. Unattended diarrhoea can lead to your dog becoming dehydrated and extremely ill.

FITS: There are a considerable number of reasons why dogs fit. Puppies that are infested with worms can fit. Once de-wormed they never fit again. Puppies may also have a reaction to their vaccinations and this can bring on a fit. This is rare but you should report it to your vet. He should be able to correct the problem. A fitting dog can be a very distressing sight. He may collapse, and may froth at the mouth. He may also go rigid and his legs may start to move as though he was running. He may also lose control over his bladder and bowels. While this is happening do not interfere, but ensure the dog can do no harm to himself while thrashing about. When the dog comes out of a fit he will be extremely weak and confused and will stand and walk as if drunk. Put the dog, at this point, in a safe, enclosed, darkened

place where he will be quiet until he has recovered. If the dog has another fit you should definitely take him to your vet. If epilepsy is diagnosed there are drugs that will control it.

HEATSTROKE: This is an acute emergency which happens during hot weather. It mostly occurs in dogs that have been shut inside a hot car. A dog should never be put in a hot car in warm weather, even with the windows well open. A car will turn into an oven on a warm day and the temperature inside the car will increase rapidly. A dog can become severely distressed in minutes and die very, very quickly. Even on much cooler days the windows must be left wide open and grills fitted. A heatstroke victim will be severely distressed, frantically panting and will probably collapse. His temperature will be extremely high and, to bring it down, the dog's body should be submerged in cool water or hosed down with water. Do not use very cold water as this will cause more problems. When the temperature returns to normal the dog should be dried and put in a cool place to recover. The dog should have drinking water available at all stages, preferably with salt added (one dessertspoonful of salt per litre of water). If the dog does not recover quickly it would be advisable to take him to the vet as he may be suffering from shock.

ABOVE: *If your dog is lame for more than two days, take him to the vet.*

LAMENESS: Dogs will go lame for many reasons but the most common causes are found in the foot. If your dog is lame, check the pads for cuts, cracks, dried mud between the pads, thistles or any kind of swelling. Check the nails have not been damaged or that the nailbed is not infected. Sores between the pads can also cause lameness. If you find a foreign body in the foot, remove it and clean the foot with warm antiseptic water. An infected nailbed will need antibiotic treatment from the vet. This condition is very painful and should be treated quickly. If it isn't treated, the nail can drop off, which can cause further serious problems. A damaged nail, if down to the nailbed, should be bandaged to stop the dog knocking it further. Be extremely careful when you bandage your dog's feet. This can do serious harm if it is done incorrectly. Get professional help if in doubt.

If nothing appears wrong in the foot you must start to go up the leg, feeling for any swellings, lumps or cuts. Feel the opposite leg and compare the shape and size. Find out if there is any difference in the heat of the legs; bend the joints and move the leg. The dog may or may not flinch when you touch the injury. Some dogs will be lame one day and, after resting overnight, will be completely sound the next. However, if the cause of your dog's lameness is still undetected and has not improved after two days you should take him to your vet.

Summary

Modern Cavaliers can trace their ancestry back to the sixteenth century to the little "comfort" spaniels favoured by aristocratic ladies. But these spirited little dogs were also taken hunting by the Duke of Marlborough who maintained that they could keep up with his trotting horse. The breed was finally recognized by the British Kennel Club in 1945 and by the American Kennel Club in 1995.

Since then, Cavaliers have become increasingly popular around the world. They are a convenient size, flexible, good natured and intelligent, all of which makes them an ideal companion and family dog. Cavaliers are also relatively low-maintenance and happy to fit it with other dogs and pets. The sweet faces and luminous eyes of these lovely dogs make them welcome wherever they go!